Manuale Precum

ALUMNORUM

Seminarii Sancti Thomae

COMPILED FROM APPROVED SOURCES
by a
Member of the
Faculty

Catholic Authors Press
www.CatholicAuthors.com

Imprimatur

† MAURITIUS FRANCISCUS McAULIFFE

Episcopus Hartfordiensis

First published in 1934
Copyright 2006 Catholic Authors Press

ISBN: 978-0-9789432-5-7

Catholic Authors Press

www.CatholicAuthors.com

CONTENTS

	Page
Special Prayers	4
Prime	9
Morning Prayers	14
Compline	21
Evening Prayers	28
Special Prayers	34
Itinerarium	36
Benedictio Mensae	37
Prayers Before Communion	41
Prayers After Communion	45
Manner of Serving at Mass	50
Serving at Mass	63
Catholic Missions	68

DE PROFUNDIS

(Psalmus 129)

De profundis clamavi ad te, Domine:° Domine, exaudi vocem meam.

Fiant aures tuæ intendentes,° in vocem deprecationis meæ.

Si iniquitates observaveris, Domine,° Domine, quis sustinebit?

Quia apud te propitiatio est,° et propter legem tuam sustinui te, Domine.

Sustinuit anima mea in verbo ejus:° speravit anima mea in Domino.

A custodia matutina usque ad noctem,° speret Israel in Domino.

Quia apud Dominum misericordia,° et copiosa apud eum redemptio.

Et ipse redimet Israel,° ex omnibus iniquitatibus ejus.

V. Requiem æternam dona eis, Domine.
R. Et lux perpetua luceat eis.
V. Requiescant in pace.
R. Amen.
V. Domine, exaudi orationem meam.
R. Et clamor meus ad te veniat.
V. Dominus vobiscum.
R. Et cum spiritu tuo.

Fidelium Deus omnium Conditor et Redemptor, animabus famulorum famularumque tuarum remissionem cunctorum tribue peccatorum: ut indulgentiam, quam semper optaverunt, piis supplicationibus consequantur. Qui vivis et regnas in sæcula sæculorum. R. Amen.

THE ANGELUS DOMINI

Angelus Domini nuntiavit Mariae:
Et concepit de Spiritu Sancto.
Ave Maria gratia plena Dominus tecum benedicta tu in mulieribus et benedictus fructus ventris tui, Jesus.
Sancta Maria, mater Dei, ora pro nobis peccatoribus nunc et in hora mortis nostrae. Amen.
Ecce ancilla Domini.
Fiat mihi secundum verbum tuum.
Ave Maria, etc.
Et verbum caro factum est..
Et habitavit in nobis.
Ave Maria, etc.
Ora pro nobis Sancta Dei Genetrix: ut digni efficiamur promissionibus Christi.

Oremus.

Gratiam tuam, quæsumus, Domine, mentibus nostris infunde: ut qui, angelo nuntiante, Christi Filii tui incarnationem cognovimus, per passionem ejus et crucem ad resurrectionis gloriam perducamur. Per eumden Christum Dominum nostrum. Amen.

REGINA COELI

Regina coeli lætare. Alleluia.
Quia quem meruisti portare. Alléluia.
Resurrexit secut dixit. Alleluia.
Ora pro nobis Deum, Alleluia.
Gaude et lætare Virgo Maria   Alleluia.
Quia surrexit Dominus vere   Alleluia.

Oremus

Deus, qui per Resurrectionem Filii tui Domini

nostri Jesu Christi mundum lætificare dignatus es; præsta, quæsumus; ut per ejus genitricem Virginem Mariam perpetuæ capiamus gaudia vitæ. Per eundem Christum Dominum nostrum. Amen.

MISERERE

Psalmus 50.

Miserere mei, Deus,° secundum magnam misericordiam tuam:

Et secundum multitudinem miserationum tuarum,° dele iniquitatem meam.

Amplius lava me ab iniquitate mea:° et a peccato meo munda me:

Quoniam iniquitatem meam ego cognosco:° et peccatum meum contra me est semper.

Tibi soli peccavi, et malum coram te feci:° ut justificeris in sermonibus tuis, et vincas cum judicaris.

Ecce enim in iniquitatibus conceptus sum;° et in peccatis concepit me mater mea.

Ecce enim veritatem dilexisti: incerta et occulta sapientiæ tuae Manifestasti Mihi.

Asperges me hyssopo, et mundabor:° lavabis me, et super nivem dealbabor.

Audituit meo dabis gaudium et lætitiam:° et exultabunt ossa humiliata.

Averte faciem tuam a peccatis meis:° et omnes iniquitates meas dele.

Cor mundum crea in me, Deus:° et spiritum rectum innova in visceribus meis.

Ne projicias me a facie tua:° et Spiritum sanctum tuum ne auferas a me.

Redde mihi lætitiam Salutaris tui:° et Spiritu principali confirma me.

Docebo iniquos vias tuas:° et impii ad te convertentur.

Libera me de sanguinibus, Deus, Deus, salutis meæ:° et exultabit lingua mea justitiam tuam.

Domine, labia mea aperies:° et os meum annuntiabit laudem tuam.

Quoniam si voluisses sacrificium, dedissem utique:° holocaustis non delectaberis.

Sacrificium Deo spiritus contribulatus:° cor contritum et humiliatum, Deus, non despicies.

Benigne fac, Domine, in bona voluntate tua Sion,° ut ædificentur muri Jerusalem.

Tunc acceptabis sacrificium justitiæ, oblationes et holocausta:° tunc imponent super altare tuum vitulos.

ANTE QUODVIS OPUS IN PARTICULARI.

Actiones nostras, quæsumus Domine, aspirando præveni et adjuvando prosequere, ut cuncta nostra oratio et operatio a te semper incipiat, et per te cœpta. finiatur. Per Christum Dominum nostrum. Amen.

(In fine:) Agimus tibi gratias,° omnipotens Deus, pro universis beneficiis tuis. Oui vivis et regnas in sæcula sæculorum. Amen.

THE MYSTERIES OF THE HOLY ROSARY

JOYFUL MYSTERIES—Monday and Thursday
1. The Annunciation.
2. The Visitation.
3. The Birth of Our Lord.

4. The Presentation of Our Lord.
5. Jesus in the Temple.

SORROWFUL MYSTERIES—Tuesday and Friday

1. The Agony in the Garden.
2. The Scourging at the Pillar.
3. The Crowning with Thorns.
4. The Carrying of the Cross.
5. The Crucifixion.

THE GLORIOUS MYSTERIES—Sunday, Wednesday and Saturday.

1. The Resurrection.
2. The Ascension.
3. The Descent of the Holy Ghost upon the Disciples.
4. The Assumption of the Blessed Virgin Mary.
5. The Crowning of the Blessed Virgin.

Hail, Holy Queen, Mother of Mercy, our life, our sweetness and our hope. To thee do we cry, poor banished children of Eve, to thee do we send up our sighs, mourning and weeping in this valley of tears. Turn then, most gracious advocate, thine eyes of mercy towards us; and after this our exile show unto us the blessed fruit of thy womb, Jesus. O clement, O loving, O sweet Virgin Mary.

V. Pray for us, O holy Mother of God.
R. That we may be made worthy of the promises of Christ.

Let Us Pray

O, God, whose only begotten Son, by His life, death and resurrection, hath purchased the reward of eternal life: grant we beseech Thee, that, meditating on these mysteries in the Most Holy Rosary of the Blessed Virgin Mary, we may imitate what they contain, and obtain what they promise. Through the same Jesus Christ, Our Lord. Amen.

PRIME *(One Psalm)*

Our Father. Hail Mary.
V. O God, come to my assistance.
R. O Lord, make haste to help me. Glory be...
Alleluia (Praise be to Thee).

Hymn

Now that the daylight fills the sky
We lift our hearts to God on high,
That He, in all we do or say,
Would keep us free from harm today:

Would guard our hearts and tongues from strife;
From anger's din would hide our life;
From evil sights would turn our eyes;
Would close our ears to vanities.

So we, when this new day is gone
And night in turn is drawing on,
With conscience by the world unstained
Shall praise His Name for victory gained.

To God the Father and the Son
And Holy Spirit, three in one,
Be endless glory as before
The world began, so evermore. Amen.
Ant. Alleluia.

Psalm 118:1-8   *The Law and its blessings*

Fidelity in God's service

Blessed are the undefiled in the way, * who walk in
the law of the Lord.

Blessed are they that search His testimonies, * who
seek Him with their whole heart.

For they that work iniquity * do not walk in His ways.

Thou hast given Thy commandments, * that they be
well observed.

Oh that my ways be well directed * unto the keeping of Thy statutes!

Then shall I not be put to shame, * when I pay heed to all Thy Precepts.

I will praise Thee with an upright heart, * for I have learnt Thy righteous judgments.

I will keep Thy justifications; * only do not Thou forsake me!

Ant. Alleluia, alleluia, alleluia.

Chap. 1 Tim. 1:17 To the King of ages, immortal, invisible, the only God, be honor and glory forever and ever. Amen.
R. Thanks be to God.
V. Arise, O Christ, and help us.
R. And deliver us for Thy Name's sake.
Lord, have mercy on us. Christ, have mercy on us. Lord, have mercy on us.
Our Father *silently.*
V. And lead us not into temptation.
R. But deliver us from evil.
V. O Lord, hear my prayer.
R. And let my cry come unto Thee.

Prayer Let us pray: O Lord God Almighty, who hast brought us to the beginning of this day, preserve us in the same by Thy power, that during this day we may not fall into any sin, but that all our words, thoughts and works may be directed to the doing of Thy righteousness. Through our Lord Jesus Christ, Thy Son, who liveth and reigneth with Thee in the unity of the Holy Ghost, God, world without end.
R. Amen.
V. O Lord, hear my prayer.
R. And let my cry come unto Thee.
V. Let us bless the Lord.
R. Thanks be to God.

The Martyrology may here be read, as at choir, at the end of which is said **Thanks be to God**

PRIME

whereupon these prayers follow

   V. Precious in the sight of the Lord.
   R. Is the death of His faithful ones.

Prayer May holy Mary and all the Saints plead for us with the Lord, that we may be helped and saved by Him who liveth and reigneth forever and ever.
   R. Amen.
   V. O God, come to my assistance.
   R. O Lord, make haste to help me.

This versicle and response is repeated three times, and then is added

Glory be to the Father and to the Son and to the Holy Ghost; / as it was in the beginning, is now and ever shall be, world without end. Amen.

Lord, have mercy on us. Christ, have mercy on us. Lord, have mercy on us.

Our Father *silently*
   V. And lead us not into temptation.
   R. But deliver us from evil.
   V. Look down upon Thy servants, O Lord, and upon the works of Thy hands, and direct their children.
   R. And let the glorious beauty of the Lord our God be upon us, and direct Thou the work of our hands over us; O do Thou direct the work of our hands. Glory be to the Father...

Prayer Let us pray: O Lord God, King of heaven and earth, may it please Thee this day to direct and sanctify, to rule and govern our hearts and bodies, our thoughts, words and deeds according to Thy law and in the doing of Thy commandments, that now and forever we may by Thy help attain salvation and freedom, O Savior of the world, who livest and reignest forever and ever.
   R. Amen.
   V. Pray, Lord, a blessing.
Blessing May the Lord Almighty order our days and deeds in His peace.
   R. Amen.

From the octave of the Epiphany until the first Sunday of Lent, and from the octave of Pentecost until Advent, exclusively.

Lesson 2 Thess. *3:5* **May the Lord direct our hearts and bodies in the love of God and the patience of Christ.**
R. **Thanks be to God.**

From the first Sunday of Advent until Christmas Eve.

Lesson Is. *33:2* **O Lord, have mercy on us, for we have waited for Thee; be Thou our defense in the morning, our salvation also in the time of trouble.**
R. **Thanks be to God.**

From the first Sunday of Lent until Passion Sunday

Lesson Is. *55:6* **Seek ye the Lord while He may be found; call ye upon Him while He is near.**
R. **Thanks be to God.**

From Passion Sunday until Holy Thursday

Lesson Is. *50:6-7* **I turned not my face from them that rebuked me and spit upon me. The Lord God is my helper, therefore am I not confounded.**
R. **Thanks be to God.**

From Easter Sunday until the Vigil of the Ascension

Lesson Col. *3:1-2* **If you be risen with Christ, seek the things that are above, where Christ is sitting at the right hand of God; mind the things that are above, not the things that are upon the earth.**
R. **Thanks be to God.**

After the lesson

V. **Our help is in the Name of the Lord.**
R. **Who made heaven and earth.**

Blessing **May the Lord bless us and defend us from all evil, and bring us to life everlasting. And may the souls of the faithful departed through the mercy of God rest in peace.**
R. **Amen.**

Let us make a remembrance of all our departed brethren, friends and benefactors.
V. May they rest in peace.
R. Amen.

Psalm 129

Out of the depths I cry to Thee, O Lord, * Lord, hear my prayer.
Let Thine ears give heed * to the voice of my supplication.
If Thou, O Lord, rememberest sins, * O Lord, who shall endure?
But with Thee is merciful forgiveness, * and for Thy law I trust in Thee, O Lord.
My soul trusteth in His word, * my soul hopeth in the Lord.
From the morning watch even to the night * let Israel hope in the Lord;
For with the Lord is mercy, * and with Him plentiful redemption;
And He shall redeem Israel * from all his iniquities.
Eternal rest grant unto them, O Lord; * and let perpetual light shine upon them.
V. From the gate of hell.
R. Deliver their souls, O Lord.
V. May they rest in peace.
R. Amen.
V. O Lord, hear my prayer.
R. And let my cry come unto Thee.

Prayer Let us pray: O God, who grantest forgiveness and desirest the salvation of mankind, we beseech Thee in Thy mercy to grant that the brethren of our congregation and their relatives and benefactors, who have passed out of this life, may partake of everlasting bliss by the intercession of blessed Mary ever Virgin and of all Thy Saints. Through our Lord Jesus Christ, Thy Son, who liveth and reigneth with Thee in the unity of the Holy Ghost, God, world without end.
R. Amen.
V. Eternal rest grant unto them, O Lord.
R. And let perpetual light shine upon them.
V. May they rest in peace.
R. Amen.

MORNING PRAYERS

In the name of the Father, and of the Son, and of the Holy Ghost. Amen.

Place Yourself in the Presence of God, and adore His holy Name.

Most holy and adorable Trinity, one God in three Persons, I believe that Thou art here present: I adore I adore Thee with the deepest humility, and render to Thee, with my whole heart, the homage which is due to Thy sovereign majesty.

AN ACT OF FAITH

O my God, I firmly believe that Thou art one God in three divine Persons, Father, Son, and Holy Ghost; I believe that Thy divine Son became man, and died for our sins, and that He will come to judge the living and the dead. I believe these and all the truths which the holy Catholic Church teaches, because Thou hast revealed them, who canst neither deceive nor be deceived.

AN ACT OF HOPE

O my God, relying on Thy infinite goodness and promises, I hope to obtain pardon of my sins, the help of Thy grace, and life everlasting, through the merits of Jesus Christ, my Lord and Redeemer.

AN ACT OF LOVE

O my God, I love Thee above all things, with my whole heart and soul, because Thou art all good and worthy of all love. I love my neighbor as myself for the love of Thee. I forgive all who have injured me, and ask pardon of all whom I have injured.

Thank God for All Favors and Offer Yourself to Him.

O my God, I most humbly thank Thee for all the favors Thou hast bestowed upon me to the present moment. I give Thee thanks from the bottom of my heart that Thou hast created me after Thine own image and likeness, that Thou hast redeemed me by the precious blood of Thy dear Son, and that Thou hast preserved me and brought me safe to the beginning of another day. I offer to Thee, O Lord, my whole being, and in particular all my thoughts, words, actions, and sufferings of this day. I consecrate them all to the glory of Thy name, beseeching Thee that through the infinite merits of Jesus Christ my Saviour they may all find acceptance in Thy sight. May Thy divine love animate them, and may they all tend to Thy greater glory.

Resolve to Avoid Sin and to Practise Virtue.

Adorable Jesus, my Saviour and Master, model of all perfection, I resolve and will endeavor this day to imitate Thy example, to be, like Thee, mild, humble, chaste, zealous, charitable, and resigned. I will redouble my efforts that I may not fall this day into any of those sins which I have heretofore committed (*here name any besetting sin*), and which I sincerely desire to forsake.

Ask God for the Necessary Graces.

O my God, Thou knowest my poverty and weakness, and that I am unable to do anything good without Thee; deny me not, O God, the help of Thy grace, proportion it to my necessities; give me strength to avoid anything evil which Thou forbiddest, and to practise the good which Thou hast commanded; and enable me to bear patiently all the trials which it may please Thee to send me.

THE LORD'S PRAYER

Pater noster, qui es in cœlis, sanctificetur nomen tuum; adveniat regnum tuum fiat voluntas tua, sicut in cœlo, et in terra. Panem nostrum quotidianum da nobis hodie; et dimitte nobis debita nostra, sicut et nos dimittimus debitoribus nostris. Et ne nos inducas in tentationem: sed libera nos a malo. Amen.

Our Father, who art in heaven, hallowed be Thy name: Thy kingdom come: Thy will be done on earth, as it is in heaven. Give us this day our daily bread: and forgive us our trespasses, as we forgive those who trespass against us. And lead us not into temptation: but deliver us from evil. Amen.

THE HAIL MARY

Ave, Maria, gratia plena: Dominus tecum: benedicta tu in mulieribus. et benedictus fructus ventris tui, Jesus. Sancta Maria, Mater Dei, ora pro nobis peccatoribus, nunc et in hora mortis nostræ. Amen.

Hail, Mary, full of grace; the Lord is with thee; blessed art thou among women, and blessed is the fruit of Thy womb, Jesus. Holy Mary, Mother of God, pray for us sinners, now and at the hour of our death. Amen.

THE APOSTLE'S CREED

Credo in Deum, Patrem omnipotentem, Creatorem cœli et terræ; et in Jesum Christum, Filium ejus unicum, Dominum nostrum; qui conceptus est de Spiritu Sancto, natus ex Maria Virgine, passus sub Pontio Pilato, crucifixus, mortuus et sepultus. Descendit ad infernos; tertia die resurrexit a mortuis; ascendit ad cœlos, sedet ad dexteram Dei Patris omnipotentis; inde venturus est judicare vivos et mortuos. Credo in Spiritum Sanctum, sanctam Ecclesiam

Catholicam, sanctorum communionem, remissionem peccatorum, carnis resurrectionem, vitam æternam. Amen.

I believe in God, the Father Almighty, Creator of heaven and earth; and in Jesus Christ, His only Son, our Lord: who was conceived by the Holy Ghost, born of the Virgin Mary, suffered under Pontius Pilate, was crucified, died, and was buried. He descended into hell; the third day He rose again from the dead; He ascended into heaven, and sitteth at the right hand of God, the Father Almighty; from thence He shall come to judge the living and the dead. I believe in the Holy Ghost, the holy Catholic Church, the communion of saints, the forgiveness of sins, the resurrection of the body, and life everlasting. Amen.

Ask the Prayers of the Blessed Virgin, your Guardian Angel, and your Patron Saint.

Holy Virgin, Mother of God, my Mother and Patroness, I place myself under thy protection. I throw myself with confidence into the arms of thy compassion. Be to me, O Mother of mercy, my refuge in distress, my consolation under suffering, my advocate with thy adorable Son, now and at the hour of my death.

    Angel of God, my guardian dear,
    To whom His love commits me here,
    Ever this day be at my side,
    To light and guard, to rule and guide.
                                     Amen.

O great Saint whose name I bear, protect me, pray for me, that like thee I may serve God faithfully on earth, and glorify Him eternally with thee in heaven. Amen.

LITANY OF THE MOST HOLY NAME OF JESUS

V. *Lord have mercy on us.*
R. { *Christ have mercy on us.*
{ *Lord have mercy on us.*
V. *Jesus hear us.*
R. *Jesus graciously hear us.*

God, the Father of heaven, *Have mercy on us.*
God the Son, Redeemer of the world, *Have, etc.*
God the Holy Ghost,
Holy Trinity, one God,
Jesus, son of the living God,
Jesus, splendor of the Father,
Jesus, brightness of eternal light,
Jesus, king of glory,
Jesus, sun of justice,
Jesus, son of the Virgin Mary,
Jesus, most amiable,
Jesus, most admirable,
Jesus, mighty God,
Jesus, father of the world to come,
Jesus, angel of the great council,
Jesus, most powerful,
Jesus, most patient,
Jesus, most obedient,
Jesus, meek and humble of heart,
Jesus, lover of chasity,
Jesus, lover of us,
Jesus, God of peace,
Jesus, author of life,
Jesus, model of virtues,
Jesus, zealous for souls,
Jesus, our God,
Jesus, our refuge,
Jesus, father of the poor,

MORNING PRAYERS

Jesus, treasure of the faithful,
Jesus, good shepherd,
Jesus, true light,
Jesus, eternal wisdom,
Jesus, infinite goodness,
Jesus, our way and our life,
Jesus, joy of angels,
Jesus, king of patriarchs,
Jesus, master of apostles,
Jesus, teacher of evangelists,
Jesus. strength of martyrs,
Jesus, light of confessors,
Jesus, purity of virgins,
Jesus, crown of all saints,

Be merciful,

Spare us, O Jesus,

Be merciful,

Graciously hear us, O Jesus

From all evil,   *Deliver us, O Jesus*
From all sin,
From Thy wrath,
From the snares of the devil,
From the spirit of fornication,
From everlasting death,
From the neglect of Thy inspirations,
Through the mystery of Thy holy incarnation,
Through Thy nativity,
Through Thine infancy,
Through Thy most divine life,
Through Thy labors,
Through Thine agony and passion,
Through Thy cross and dereliction,
Through Thy faintness and weariness,
Through Thy death and burial,
Through Thy resurrection,

Through Thine ascension,
Through the institution of Thy most Holy Eucharist.
Through Thy joys,
Through Thy glory,

Lamb of God, who takest away the sins of the world
Spare us, O Jesus,

Lamb of God, who takest away the sins of the world
Graciously hear us, O Jesus.

Lamb of God, who takest away the sins of the world
Have mercy on us, O Jesus.

Jesus, hear us.
Jesus, graciously hear us.

Have mercy on us.

O Lord Jesus Christ, who hast said: Ask, and ye shall receive; seek, and ye shall find; knock, and it shall be opened unto you; grant, we beseech Thee, unto us who ask, the gift of Thy most divine love, that we may ever love Thee with all our hearts, and in all our words and actions, and never cease from showing forth Thy praise.

Make us, O Lord, to have a perpetual fear and love of Thy holy Name; for Thou never failest to govern those whom Thou dost solidly establish in Thy love. Who livest and reignest, world without end. Amen.

Indulgence of 300 days, once a day. Leo XIII. Jan. 16, 1886.

COMPLINE

Blessing May Almighty God grant us a peaceful night and a perfect end.

R. Amen.

Lesson 1 Pet. 5:8-9 Be prudent and watch because your adversary the devil as a roaring lion goeth about seeking whom he may devour, whom resist ye, strong in faith.

R. Thanks be to God.

V. Our help is in the Name of the Lord.

R. Who made heaven and earth.

Confiteor (in unison) I confess to Almighty God, * to blessed Mary ever Virgin, to blessed Michael the Archangel, / to blessed John the Baptist, to the holy Apostles Peter and Paul, / and to all the Saints, / that I have sinned exceedingly in thought, word and deed: / through my fault, through my fault, through my most grievous fault. / Therefore I pray blessed Mary ever Virgin, blessed Michael the Archangel, / blessed John the Baptist, the holy Apostles Peter and Paul, / and all the Saints / to pray to the Lord our God for me.

Absolution May Almighty God have mercy on us, forgive us our sins and bring us to life everlasting.

R. Amen.

May the Almighty and merciful Lord grant us pardon, absolution and remission of our sins.

R. Amen.

V. Convert us, O God our Savior.

R. And turn away Thy anger from us.

V. O God, come to my assistance.

R. O Lord, make haste to help me. Glory be...
Alleluia (Praise be to Thee).

Psalm 33 *Blessings of holy fear*

I will bless the Lord for ever, * His praise be always in my mouth.

My soul shall glory in the Lord; * the poor shall hear it and rejoice.

Sing praise to the Lord with me, * and together let us celebrate His name!

I have sought the Lord and He hath heard me, * He hath delivered me from all my troubles;

Come near to Him and be enlightened, * and your faces will not be ashamed.

The poor man cried and the Lord heard him, * and He saved him from all his tribulations.

The angel of the Lord hovers over them that fear Him,* and he delivereth them.

O taste and see, that the Lord is sweet; * blessed the man who hopeth in Him!

Fear the Lord, all ye His saints, * for they suffer no want who fear Him;

The rich suffer need and hunger; * but those who seek the Lord do not lack good things.

Glory be to the Father (etc.)

Come, my children, hearken to me; * I will teach you the fear of the Lord;

Who is the man that desireth life, * that loveth to see good days?

Keep thy tongue from evil, * and thy lips from speaking guile;

Turn away from evil and do good, * seek peace and pursue it.

The eyes of the Lord are upon the just, * and His ears intent upon their prayers;

But the countenance of the Lord is against the evildoers, * to wipe out their memory from the earth.

The righteous call and the Lord heareth them, * and delivereth them from all their troubles:

The Lord is nigh to the broken-hearted, * and the lowly in spirit He doth save.

Many are the afflictions of the just, * but the Lord delivereth them from all;

The Lord protecteth all their bones; * not one of them shall be broken.

Most wretched is the death of sinners; * and they that hate the just shall suffer.

The Lord keepeth the life of His servants, * and all who trust in Him, will not fail.

Glory be to the Father (etc.)

Psalm 60

Hear O God my supplication: be attentive to my prayer.

To Thee have I cried from the ends of the earth: when my heart was in anguish thou hast exalted me on a rock.

Thou hast conducted me; for Thou hast been my hope: a tower of strength against the face of the enemy.

In Thy tabernacle I dwell forever: I shall be protected under the covert of Thy wings.

For Thou, my God, has heard my prayer: Thou hast given an inheritance to them that fear Thy name.

Thou wilt add days to the days of the king: his years even to generation and generation.

He abideth forever in the sight of God, his mercy and truth who shall search?

So will I sing a psalm to Thy name forever and ever: that I may pay my vows from day to day.

Glory be to the Father (etc.)

COMPLINE

Hymn

To Thee, before the close of day,
Creator of the world, we pray
That with Thy wonted favor Thou
Wouldst be our Guard and Keeper now.

From evil dreams defend our eyes,
From nightly fears and fantasies;
Tread under foot our ghostly foe
That no pollution we may know.

O Father, grant that this be done
Through Jesus Christ Thy only Son,
Who with the Holy Ghost and Thee
Shall live and reign eternally. Amen.

Chap. Jer. 14:9 Thou, O Lord, art among us, and Thy holy Name is called upon by us; forsake us not, O Lord our God.
R. Thanks be to God.
Resp. Into Thy hands, O Lord, * I commend my spirit *which is repeated*
R. For Thou hast redeemed us, O Lord, God of truth.
I commend my spirit.
V. Glory be to the Father and to the Son and to the Holy Ghost.
Into Thy hands, O Lord, * I commend my spirit.
V. Keep us, O Lord, as the apple of Thine eye.
R. Protect us under the shadow of Thy wings.

Ant. Save us, O Lord.

Luke 2:29-32   *Canticle of Simeon*

Now dost Thou dismiss Thy servant, O Lord, * in peace, according to Thy word;

Because mine eyes have seen Thy salvation, * which Thou hast prepared in the sight of all nations,

A light of revelation to the Gentiles * and the glory of Thy people Israel. Glory be to the Father.....

Ant. Save us, O Lord, while we are awake, and keep us while we sleep, / that we may wake with Christ and rest in peace.

Lord, have mercy on us. Christ, have mercy on us. Lord, have mercy on us.

Our Father *silently*

V. And lead us not into temptation.
R. But deliver us from evil.
V. O Lord, hear my prayer.
R. And let my cry come unto Thee.

Prayer Let us pray: Visit, we beseech Thee, O Lord, this dwelling and drive far from it all snares of the enemy; let Thy holy Angels dwell herein, who may keep us in peace, and let Thy blessing be always upon us. Through our Lord Jesus Christ, Thy Son, who liveth and reigneth with Thee in the unity of the Holy Ghost, God, world without end.

R. Amen.
V. O Lord, hear my prayer.
R. And let my cry come unto Thee.
V. Let us bless the Lord.
R. Thanks be to God.

Blessing. May the Almighty and merciful Lord, Father, Son and Holy Ghost, bless and keep us.
R. Amen.

One of the following anthems of our Blessed Lady is prayed after the Office.

From the first Vespers of the first Sunday of Advent until the second Vespers of the feast of the Purification, inclusively.

Loving Mother of our Redeemer, / thou gate leading to heaven and star of the sea: / help thy falling people who seek to rise, / thou who, all nature wondering, didst give birth to thy holy Creator: / Virgin always, hearing that greeting from Gabriel's lips, / take pity on sinners.

V. during Advent The Angel of the Lord declared unto Mary.
R. And she conceived of the Holy Ghost.

Prayer Let us pray: Pour forth, we beseech Thee, O Lord, Thy grace into our hearts, that we to whom the incarnation of Christ Thy Son was made known by the message of an Angel, may by His passion and Cross be brought to the glory of the resurrection. Through the same Christ our Lord.
R. Amen.

V. from the first Vespers of Christmas After childbirth thou didst remain an inviolate Virgin.
R. Mother of God, pray for us.

Prayer Let us pray: O God, who by the fruitful virginity of Blessed Mary hast given to mankind the rewards of eternal salvation, grant, we beseech Thee, that we may experience her intercession for us through whom we received the author of life, our Lord Jesus Christ, Thy Son.
R. Amen.

II.

From Compline of the feast of the Purification until Compline on Wednesday during Holy Week.

Hail! Queen of heaven; / hail! Lady of the Angels; / hail! root and gate from which the light of the world was born! / Rejoice glorious Virgin, fairest of all! / Farewell! most beautiful, and pray for us to Christ!
V. Grant that I may praise thee, O holy Virgin.
R. Give me strength against thy enemies.

Prayer Let us pray: Grant, O merciful God, help to our weakness, that we who commemorate the holy Mother of God, may by the help of her intercession rise from our sins. Through the same Christ our Lord.
R. Amen.

III.

From Compline on Holy Saturday until None on the Saturday after Pentecost

Queen of heaven, rejoice, alleluia! / for He whom thou wast chosen to bear, alleluia! / has risen as He said, alleluia! / Pray for us to God, alleluia.
 V. Rejoice and be glad, O Virgin Mary, alleluia!
 R. For the Lord is truly risen, alleluia!

Prayer Let us pray: O God, who didst deign to give joy to the world through the resurrection of Thy Son our Lord Jesus Christ, grant, we beseech Thee, that through His Mother, the Virgin Mary, we may obtain the joys of everlasting life. Through the same Christ our Lord.
 R. Amen.

IV.

From the first Vespers of the feast of the Most Holy Trinity until None on the Saturday before the first Sunday of Advent.

Hail! holy Queen, / Mother of mercy, our life, our sweetness and our hope. / To thee do we cry, poor banished children of Eve. / To thee do we send up our sighs, mourning and weeping in this valley of tears. / Turn then, most gracious advocate, thine eyes of mercy towards us. / And after this our exile, show unto us the blessed fruit of thy womb, Jesus. / O clement, O loving, O sweet Virgin Mary.
 V. Pray for us, O holy Mother of God.
 R. That we may be made worthy of the promises of Christ.

Prayer Let us pray: Almighty and everlasting God, who by the co-operation of the Holy Ghost didst make ready the body and soul of the glorious Virgin and Mother Mary to be a fit dwelling for Thy Son, grant that we, who rejoice in her memory, may be freed from present ills and from eternal death by her prayers. Through the same Christ our Lord.
 R. Amen.

Last of all is said
 V. May the divine assistance remain always with us.
 R. And with our absent brethren. Amen.

EVENING PRAYERS

In the name of the Father, and of the Son, and of the Holy Ghost. Amen.

Come, O Holy Ghost, fill the hearts of Thy faithful, and kindle in them the fire of Thy love.

Place Yourself in the Presence of God

O my God, I present myself before Thee at the end of another day, to offer Thee anew the homage of my heart. I humbly adore Thee, my Creator, my Redeemer, and my Judge! I believe in Thee, because Thou art Truth itself; I hope in Thee, because Thou art faithful to Thy promises; I love Thee with my whole heart, because Thou art infinitely worthy of being loved and for Thy sake I love my neighbor as myself.

Return Thanks to God for All His Mercies.

Enable me, O my God, to return Thee thanks as I ought for all Thine inestimable blessings and favors. Thou hast thought of me and loved me from all eternity; Thou hast formed me out of nothing; Thou hast delivered up Thy beloved Son to the ignominious death of the cross for my redemption; Thou hast made me a member of Thy holy Church; Thous hast preserved me from falling into the abyss of eternal misery, when my sins had provoked Thee to punish me; Thou hast graciously continued to spare me, even though I have not ceased to offend Thee. What return, O my God, can I make for Thy innumerable blessings, and particularly for the favors of this day? O all ye saints and angels, unite with me in praising the God of mercies, who is so bountiful to so unworthy a creature.

Our Father. Hail Mary. I believe.

Ask of God Light to Discover the Sins Committed this Day.

O my God, sovereign judge of men, who desirest not the death of a sinner, but that he should be converted and saved, enlighten my mind, that I may know the sins which I have this day committed in thought, word, or deed, and give me the grace of true contrition.

Here Examine Your Conscience;

O my God, I heartily repent and am grieved that I have offended Thee, because Thou art infinitely good and sin is infinitely displeasing to Thee. I humbly ask of Thee mercy and pardon, through the infinite merits of Jesus Christ. I resolve, by the assistance of Thy grace, to do penance for my sins, and I will endeavor never more to offend Thee.

THE CONFITEOR

Confiteor Deo omnipotenti, beatæ Mariæ semper Virgini, beato Michäeli Archangelo, beato Joanni Baptistæ, sanctis apostolis Petro et Paulo, omnibus sanctis, (et tibi Pater), quia peccavi nimis cogitatione, verbo, et opere, mea culpa, mea culpa, mea maxima culpa. Ideo precor beatam Mariam semper Virginem, beatum Michäelem Archangelum, beatum Joannem Baptistam, sanctos apostolos Petrum et Paulum, omnes sanctos, (et te, Pater), orare pro me ad Dominum Deum nostrum.

Misereatur nostri Omnipotens Deus, et dimissis peccatis nostris, perducat nos ad vitam æternam. Amen.

Indulgentiam, absolutionem, et remissionem peccatorum nostrorum, tribuat nobis omnipotens et misericors Dominus. Amen.

I confess to Almighty God, to blessed Mary, ever Virgin, to blessed Michael the Archangel, to blessed John the Baptist, to the holy apostles Peter and Paul, and to all the saints (and to you, Father) that I have sinned exceedingly in thought, word, and deed, through my fault, through my fault, through my most grievous fault. Therefore I beseech blessed Mary ever Virgin, blessed Michael the Archangel, blessed John the Baptist, the holy apostles Peter and Paul, all the saints (and you, Father) to pray to the Lord our God for me.

May Almighty God have mercy upon us, and forgive us our sins, and bring us unto life everlasting. Amen.

May the Almighty and merciful Lord grant us pardon, absolution, and remission of our sins. Amen.

Pray for the Church of Christ.

O God, hear my prayers on behalf of our Holy Father Pope *N.*, our Bishop, our clergy, and for all that are in authority over us. Bless, I beseech Thee, the whole Catholic Church, and convert all heretics and unbelievers.

Prayer for the Living and for the Faithful Departed.

Pour down Thy blessings, O Lord, upon all my friends, relations, acquaintances, and benefactors and upon my enemies, if I have any. Help the poor and sick, and those who are in their last agony. O God of mercy and goodness, have compassion on the souls of the faithful in purgatory; put an end to their sufferings, and grant to them eternal light, rest, and happiness. Amen.

Commend Yourself to God, to the Blessed Virgin, and the Saints.

Bless, O Lord, the repose I am about to take, that, my bodily strength being renewed, I may be the better enabled to serve Thee.

O blessed Virgin Mary, Mother of mercy, pray for me that I may be preserved this night from all evil, whether of body or soul. Blessed St. Joseph, and all ye saints and angels of Paradise, especially my guardian angel and my chosen patron, watch over me. I commend myself to your protection now and always. Amen.

PROPAGATION OF THE FAITH PRAYERS

Our Father, Hail Mary, St. Francis Xavier, Pray for us.

LITANY OF THE BLESSED VIRGIN

V. *Lord have mercy on us.*
R. { *Christ have mercy on us.*
{ *Lord have mercy on us.*
V. *Christ hear us.*
R. *Christ graciously hear us.*

God the Father of heaven, *have mercy on us.*

God the Son, Redeemer of the world, *have mercy on us.*

God the Holy Ghost, *have mercy on us.*

Holy Trinity, one God, *have mercy on us.*

Holy Mary, *pray for us.*

Holy Mother of God,

Holy virgin of virgins,
Mother of Christ,
Mother of divine grace,
Mother most pure,
Mother most chaste,
Mother inviolate,
Mother undefiled,
Mother most amiable,
Mother most admirable,
Mother of Good Counsel,
Mother of our Creator,
Mother of our Saviour,
Virgin most prudent,
Virgin most venerable,
Virgin most renowned,
Virgin, most powerful,
Virgin most merciful,
Virgin most faithful,
Mirror of justice,
Seat of wisdom,
Cause of our joy,
Spiritual vessel,
Vessel of honor,
Singular vessel of devotion,
Mystical rose,
Tower of David,
Tower of ivory,
House of gold,
Ark of the covenant,
Gate of heaven,
Morning star,
Health of the sick,
Refuge of sinners,
Comforter of the afflicted,
Help of Christians,
Queen of angels,

Queen of patriarchs,
Queen of prophets,
Queen of apostles,
Queen of martyrs,
Queen of confessors,
Queen of virgins,
Queen of all saints,
Queen conceived without original sin,
Queen of the most holy rosary,
Queen of peace,

Lamb of God, who takest away the sins of the world, *spare us, O Lord.*

Lamb of God, who takest away the sins of the world, *graciously hear us, O Lord.*

Lamb of God, who takest away the sins of the world, *have mercy on us.*

V. Pray for us, O holy Mother of God.

R. That we may be made worthy of the promises of Christ.

Let us Pray.

Pour forth, we beseech Thee, O Lord, Thy grace into our hearts; that we, to whom the incarnation of Christ, Thy Son, was made known by the message of an angel, may, by His passion and cross, be brought to the glory of His resurrection. Through the same Christ, our Lord. Amen.

STABAT MATER

Stabat Mater dolorosa,
Juxta Crucem lacrymosa,
Dum pendebat filius.

Cujus animam gementem,
Contristatam, et dolentem,
Pertransivit gladius.

O quam tristis et afflicta
Fuit illa benedicta
Mater Unigeniti!

Quæ mœrebat, et dolebat,
Pia Mater dum videbat
Nati pœnas incliti.

Quis est homo qui non fleret,
Matrem Christi si videret
In tanto supplicio?

Quis non posset contristari?
Christi Matrem contemplari
Dolentem cum filio?

Pro peccatis suæ gentis
Vidit Jesum in tormentis,
Et flagellis subditum.

Vidit suum dulcem natum.
Moriendo desolatum,
Dum emisit spiritum.

Eia, mater, fons amoris,
Me sentire vim doloris
Fac, ut tecum lugeam.

Fac ut ardeat cor meum
In amando Christum Deum,
Ut sibi complaceam.

Sancta Mater, istud agas,
Crucifixi fige plagas
Cordi meo valide.

Tui nati vulnerati,
Tam dignati pro me pati,
Pœnas mecum divide.

Fac me tecum pie flere,
Christi, cum sit hinc exire.
Donec ego vixero.

Juxa Crucem tecum stare,
Et me tibi sociare
In planctu desidero.

Virgo virginum præclara,
Mihi jam non sis amara,
Fac me tecum plangere.

Fac ut portem Christi mortem,
Passionis fac consortem,
Et plagas recolere.

Fac me plagis vulnerari,
Fac me Cruce inebriari,
Et cruore Filii.

Flammis ne urar succensus,
Per te, Virgo, sim defensus
In die judicii.

Christe, cum sit hinc exire.
Da per matrem me venire
Ad palmam victoriæ.

Quando corpus morietur,
Fac ut animæ donetur
Paradisi gloria.
Amen.

ITINERARIUM

Clericus in ipso itineris ingressu, si solus fuerit, dicat quae sequuntur in singulari, si cum sociis, in plurali.
Ana. In viam pacis.
Canticum. Benedictus Dominus Deus Israel.
In fine Gloria Patri.
Ana. In viam pacis et prosperitatis dirigat nos omnipotens et misericors Dominus : et Angelus Raphael comitetur nobiscum in via, ut cum pace, salute, et gaudio revertamur ad propria. Kyrie eleison. Christe eleison. Kyrie eleison.

Pater noster. *secreto.*

V. Et ne nos inducas in tentationem. *R.* Sed libera nos a malo.

V. Salvos fac servos tuos. *R.* Deus meus sperantes in te.

V. Mitte nobis Domine auxilium de sancto. *R.* Et de Sion tuere nos.

V. Esto nobis Domine turris fortitudinis. *R.* A facie inimici.

V. Nihil proficiat inimicus in nobis. *R.* Et filius iniquitatis non apponat nocere nobis.

V. Benedictus Dominus die quotidie. *R.* Prosperum iter faciat nobis Deus salutarium nostrorum.

V. Vias tuas Domine demonstra nobis. *R.* Et semitas tuas edoce nos.

V. Utinam dirigantur viae nostrae. *R.* Ad custodiendas justificationes tuas.

V. Erunt prava in directa. *R.* Et aspera in vias planas.

V. Angelis suis Deus mandavit de te. *R.* Ut custodiant te in omnibus viis tuis.

V. Domine exaudi. *R.* Dominus vobiscum.
Oratio. Oremus.

Deus, qui filios Israel per maris medium sicco vestigio ire fecisti, quique tribus Magis iter ad te stella duce pandisti : tribue nobis quaesumus iter prosperum, tempusque tranquillum : ut Angelo tuo sancto comite, ad eum quo pergimus locum, ac demum ad aeternae salutis portum pervenire feliciter valeamus.

Deus, qui Abraham puerum tuum de Ur Chaldaeorum
eductum per omnes suae peregrinationis vias illaesum
custodisti : quaesumus, ut nos famulos tuos custodire
digneris : esto nobis Domine in procinc u suffragium,
in via solatium, in aestu umbraculum, in pluvia et
frigore tegumentum, in lassitudine vehiculum, in adversitate praesidium, in lubrico baculus, in naufragio portus :
ut te duce, quo tendimus, prospere perveniamus, et demum incolumes ad propria redeamus.

Adesto, quaesumus Domine, supplicationibus nostris :
et viam famulorum tuorum in salutis tuae prosperitate
dispone : ut inter omnes viae et vitae hujus varietates
tuo semper protegamur auxilio.

Praesta, quaesumus omnipotens Deus, ut familia tua
per viam salutis incedat, et beati Joannis praecursoris
hortamenta sectando, ad eum quem praedixit, secura
perveniat, Dominum nostrum Jesum Christum Filium
tuum. Qui tecum vivit et regnat.

V. Procedamus in pace. *R.* In nomine Domini.
Amen.

BENEDICTIO MENSAE

Ante prandiu Sacerdos benedicturus mensam incipit

Benedicite. *et alii repetunt.* Benedicite. *Deinde dicit V.* Oculi omnium. *et alii prosequuntur.* In
te sperant, Dne, et tu das escam illorum in tempore opportuno. Aperis tu manum tuam, et imples omne animal
benedictione. Gloria Patri. Sicut erat.

Kyrie eleison. Christe eleison. Kyrie eleison.

Pater noster. *secreto.* *V.* Et ne nos inducas in
tentationem. *R.* Sed libera nos a malo.

Postea Sacerdos dicit.
Oremus.

Benedic Domine nos et haec tua dona, quae de tua
largitate sumus sumpturi. Per Christum Dominum nostrum. *R.* Amen.

Deinde Lector. Jube domne benedicere. *Benedictio.*
Mensae coelestis participes faciat nos Rex aeternae gloriae. *R.* Amen.

SPECIAL PRAYERS

Post prandium aguntur gratiae hoc modo. Dicto a Lectore. **Tu autem Domine miserere nobis.** *R.* **Deo gratias. omnes surgunt.**

Sacerdos incipit V. **Confiteantur tibi Domine omnia opera tua.** *R.* **Et Sancti tui benedicant tibi.**

V. **Gloria Patri.** *R.* **Sicut erat.**

Postea Sacerdos absolute dicit.

Agimus tibi gratias omnipotens Deus, pro universis beneficiis tuis: Qui vivis et regnas in saceula saeculorum. *R.* Amen.

Deinde alternatim dicitur Ps. **Miserere mei Deus** *vel Ps.* **Laudate Dominum omnes Gentes.**

Gloria Patri. Sicut erat.

Kyrie eleison. Christe eleison. Kyrie eleison.

Sacerdos dicit. **Pater noster.** *secreto.*

V. Et ne nos inducas in tentationem. *R.* Sed libera nos a malo.

V. Dispersit, dedit pauperibus. *R.* Justitia ejus manet in saeculum saeculi.

V. Benedicam Dominum in omni tempore. *R.* Semper laus ejus in ore meo.

V. In Domino laudabitur anima mea. *R.* Audiant mansueti, et laetentur.

V. Magnificate Dominum mecum. *R.* Et exaltemus nomen ejus in idipsum.

V. Sit nomen Domini benedictum. *R.* Ex hoc nunc et usque in saeculum.

Deinde sine Oremus.

Retribuere dignare Domine omnibus nobis bona facientibus propter nomen tuum vitam aeternam. *R.* Amen.

V. Benedicamus Domino. *R.* Deo gratias.

V. Fidelium animae per misericordiam Dei requiescant in pace. *R.* Amen.

Pater noster. *secreto.*

Quo finito, dicit Sacerdos. Deus det nobis suam pacem. *R.* Amen.

Ante coenam Sacerdos benedicturus mensam incipit. **Benedicite. et alii repetunt.** **Benedicite.**

Deinde Sacerdos incipit. V. et alii prosequuntur.

Edent pauperes, et saturabuntur, et laudabunt Dominum, qui requirunt eum : vivent corda eorum in saeculum saeculi.

SPECIAL PRAYERS 39

Gloria Patri. Sicut erat.
Kyrie eleison. Christe eleison. Kyrie eleison.
Pater noster. *secreto.*
V. Et ne nos inducas in tentationem. *R.* Sed libera nos a malo.
Oremus. Benedic Domine. *ut supra in prandio.*
Jube domne benedicere. *Bened.* Ad coenam vitae aeternae perducat nos Rex aeternae gloriae. *R.* Amen.
In fine coenae dicitur V. Memoriam fecit mirabilium suorum misericors et miserator Dominus : escam dedit timentibus se.
Gloria Patri. Sicut erat.
Sacerdos dicat.
Benedictus Deus in donis suis, et sanctus in omnibus operibus suis. Qui vivit et regnat in saecula saeculorum.
R. Amen.
Deinde alternatim dicitur Ps. Laudate Dominum. *et reliqua ut supra Quando semel comeditur, omnia dicuntur ut in coena. Praedictus modus benedicendi mensam, et agendi gratias, servatur omni tempore praeterquam diebus infrascriptis, quibus Versiculi et Psalmi tantum variantur.*
In Nativitate Dni, usque ad coenam Vigiliae Epiphaniae exclusive, dicitur.
V. Verbum caro factum est, alleluia. *R.* Et habitavit in nobis, alleluia. Gloria Patri. Sicut erat.
In fine dicitur V. Notum fecit Dominus, alleluia. *R.* Salutare suum, alleluia.
Alia ut supra. Ps. Cantate Domino canticum. *vel* Laudate Dnum omnes Gentes. *qui Psalmus semper ad beneplacitum dici potest etiam in aliis solemnitatibus.*
In Epiphania, et per totam Octav. V. Reges Tharsis et insulae munera offerent, alleluia. *R.* Reges Arabum et Saba dona adducent, alleluia. Gloria Patri.
In fine dicitur V. Omnes de Saba venient, alleluia. *R.* Aurum et thus deferentes, alleluia. Gloria Patri. *Ps.* Deus judicium.
Feria quinta in Coena Dni dicitur absolute et sine nota V. Christus factus est pro nobis obediens usque ad mortem. *Deinde* Pater noster. *totum secreto. Quo dicto, sine pronuntiatione aliqua Sacerdos signo Crucis benedicit mensam : nec dicitur.* Jube domne. *nec* Tu autem.

In fine repetitur V. **Christus factus est.** *ut supra. Postea Ps.* **Miserere mei Deus.** *Quo finito sine V.* **Gloria Patri.** *secreto dicitur* **Pater noster.**

Deinde Sacerdos dicit absolute Orat. **Respice, quaesumus.** *ut in Breviario hac die. Non pronuntiatur.* **Qui tecum.** *nec* **Fidelium animae.** *sed secreto dicitur* **Pater noster.** *nec additur* **Deus det nobis suam pacem.**

In Parasceve eodem modo fit sicut in Coena Domini, sed additur ad V. **Christus factus est. Mortem autem crucis.**

Sabbato sancto ad benedicendum mensam dicitur **Benedicite.** *R.* **Benedicite.**

V. **Vespere autem sabbati, quae lucescit in prima sabbati, alleluia.** *V.* **Venit Maria Magdalene, et altera Maria videre sepulcrum, alleluia. Gloria Patri. Sicut erat.**

PREPARATION FOR HOLY COMMUNION

Prayer of St. Ambrose

O Gracious Lord Jesus Christ, I, a sinner, in no way presuming on my own deserts, but trusting in Thy mercy and goodness, with fear and trembling approach the Table of Thy most sweet Feast. For my heart and body are stained with many sins; my thoughts and lips have not been diligently guarded. Wherefore, O gracious God, O awful Majesty, in my extremity I turn to Thee, the Fount of Mercy; to Thee I hasten to be healed, and take refuge under Thy protection; and for Thee, before whom I cannot stand as my Judge, I long as my Savior. To Thee, O Lord, I show my wounds, to Thee I lay bare my shame. I know my sins are many and great, for which I am afraid. My trust is in Thy mercies, of which there is no end. Look therefore upon me with the eyes of Thy mercy, O Lord Jesus Christ. God and Man, crucified for mankind; hearken unto me, whose trust is in Thee; have mercy upon me, who am full of sin and misery, O Thou fount of mercy, that wilt never cease to flow. Hail, saving Victim, offered for me and all mankind on the Cross of suffering and shame. Hail, noble and precious Blood, flowing from the wounds of my crucified Lord and Savior Jesus Christ, and washing away the sins of the whole world. Be mindful, O Lord, of Thy creature, whom Thou hast redeemed with Thine own Blood. I repent of my sins. I desire to amend. Take therefore away from me, O most merciful Father, all my iniquities: that, being cleansed both in body and soul, I may worthily taste the Holy of Holies; and grant that this holy partaking of Thy Body and Blood, which, unworthy as I am, I purpose to receive, may be for the remission of my sins, and the perfect cleansing of all my offences, for the driving away of all evil thoughts and the renewal of all holy desires, for the healthful bringing forth of fruit well-pleasing unto Thee, and the most sure protection of my soul and body against the snares of my enemies. Amen. (100 days' Indulgence.)

Prayer of St. Thomas

Almighty, everlasting God, behold, I draw near to the Sacrament of Thine Only-begotton Son, our Lord Jesus Christ. As sick, I approach to the Physician of Life; unclean, to the Fountain of Mercy; blind, to the Light of eternal Brightness; poor and needy, to the Lord of heaven and earth. I implore Thee, therefore, out of the abundance of Thy boundless mercy, that Thou wouldst vouchsafe to heal my sickness, to wash my defilements, to enlighten my blindness, to enrich my poverty, and to clothe my nakedness; that I may receive the Bread of Angels, the King of kings, the Lord of lords, with such reverence and humility, such contrition and devotion, such purity and faith, such purpose and intention, as to be expedient for the health of my soul. Grant, I beseech Thee, that I may receive not only the Sacrament of the Body and Blood of the Lord, but also the whole grace and virtue of that Sacrament. O most merciful God, grant me so to receive the Body of Thine Only-begotten Son, our Lord Jesus Christ, which He took of the Virgin Mary, that I may be found worthy to be incorporated into His mystical Body, and accounted among His members And, O most loving Father, grant that whom I now purpose to receive under a veil I may at last behold with unveiled face, even Thy beloved Son, Who with Thee and the Holy Ghost ever liveth and reigneth, one God, world without end. Amen. (100 days' Indulgence.)

Prayer to the Blessed Virgin

O Most Blessed Virgin Mary, mother of gentleness and mercy, I, a miserable and unworthy sinner, fly to thy protection with every sentiment of humility and love; and I implore of thy loving kindness that thou wouldst vouchsafe graciously to be near me, and all who throughout the whole Church are to receive the Body and Blood of thy Son this day, even as thou wert near thy sweetest Son as He hung bleeding on the Cross: that, aided by thy gracious help, we may worthily offer up a pure and acceptable sacrifice in the sight of the Holy and Undivided Trinity. Amen. (100 days' Indulgence.)

Prayer to St. Joseph

Happy and blessed art thou, O Joseph, to whom it was given not only to see that God whom many kings desired to see, and saw not, to hear, and heard not; but also to hear Him in thine arms, to embrace Him, to clothe Him, and to guard and defend Him.

V. Pray for us, O Blessed Joseph.

R. That we may be made worthy of the promises of Christ.

Let Us Pray

O God, who hast given unto us a Royal Priesthood, vouchsafe, we beseech Thee, that as Blessed Joseph was found worthy to handle with his hands, and bear within his arms, Thine Only-begotten Son, born of the Virgin Mary, so may we be made fit, by cleanness of heart and innocency of works to wait upon Thy holy Altars; that we may worthily receive the Most Sacred Body and Blood of Thy Son, now in this present life, and deserve to attain an everlasting reward in the world to come. Through the same Christ our Lord. Amen. (100 days' Indulgence.)

Prayer to all the Angels and Saints

Angels, Archangels, Thrones, Dominations, Principalities, Powers and Virtues of heaven, Cherubim and Seraphim, all ye holy Saints of God, especially my Patron Saints, deign to intercede for me, that I may worthily offer this sacrifice to God Almighty, to the praise and glory of His name, to my benefit, and for the welfare of His holy Church. Amen. (100 days' Indulgence.)

Prayer in Honor of the Saint of the Day

O Saint——————————, behold, I, a miserable sinner, trusting in thy merits, now offer the Most holy Sacrifice of the Body and Blood of our Lord Jesus Christ to thine honor and glory. I humbly and devoutly beseech thee, that thou wilt deign to intercede for me to-day, that I may offer this sublime Sacrifice in a worthy and acceptable manner, so that I may be made worthy to praise Him with thee and all His elect, and reign with Him for ever, Who liveth and reigneth world without end. Amen. (100 days' Indulgence.)

Direction of the Intention

I intend to offer the Holy Sacrifice of the Mass. and to receive the Body and Blood of our Lord Jesus Christ, according to the Rite of the holy Roman Church, to the praise of Almighty God and of the whole Court of Heaven; for my benefit, and that of the whole Church on earth; for all those who have commended themselves to my prayers, in general and in particular; and for the Church.

Joy with peace, amendment of life, space for true repentance, the grace and comfort of the Holy Ghost, perseverance in good works, a contrite and humble heart, and a happy consummation of my life, grant unto me, O Almighty and merciful Lord. Amen.

PRAYERS AFTER COMMUNION

Prayer of St. Thomas Aquinas

I render thanks to Thee, O Lord, Holy Father, Everlasting God, who hast vouchsafed, not for any merits of mine, but of Thy great mercy only, to feed me a sinner, Thine unworthy servant, with the precious Body and Blood of Thy Son, our Lord Jesus Christ; and I pray that this Holy Communion may not be for my judgment and condemnation, but for my pardon and salvation. Let it be unto me an armor of faith and a shield of good purpose, a riddance of all vices, and a rooting out of all evil desires; an increase of love and patience, of humility and obedience, and of all virtues, a firm defence against the wiles of all my enemies, visible and invisible; a perfect quieting of all my impulses, fleshly and spiritual; a cleaving unto Thee, the one true God; and a blessed consummation of my end when Thou dost call. And I pray that Thou wouldst vouchsafe to bring me, a sinner, to that unspeakable Feast where Thou, with Thy Son and Thy Holy Spirit, art to Thy holy ones true light, fulness of blessedness, everlasting joy, and perfect happiness. Through the same Christ our Lord. Amen. (One year's Indulgence.)

Prayer of St. Bonaventure

O Most sweet Lord Jesus, transfix the affections of my inmost soul with that most joyous and healthful wound of Thy love, with true, serene, and most holy Apostolic charity, that my soul may ever languish and melt with entire love and longing for Thee, that it may desire Thee, and faint for Thy courts, long to be dissolved and to be with Thee. Grant that my soul may hunger after Thee, the Bread of Angels, the

Refreshment of holy souls, our daily and supersubstantial Bread, who hast all sweetness and savor, and the sweetness of every taste. Let my heart ever hunger after and feed upon Thee, upon whom the Angels desire to look, and my inmost soul be filled with the sweetness of Thy savor. May it ever thirst for Thee, the Fountain of life, the Source of all wisdom and knowledge, the Fountain of eternal light, the Torrent of pleasure, the Richness of the House of God. May it ever yearn for Thee, seek Thee, find Thee, stretch towards Thee, attain to Thee, meditate upon Thee, speak of Thee, and do all things to the praise and glory of Thy holy name, with humility and discretion, with love and delight, with readiness and affection, with perseverance even unto the end. And be Thou ever my hope and my whole confidence; my riches; my delight, my pleasure, and my joy; my rest and tranquillity; my peace, my sweetness, and my fragrance; my sweet savor, my food and refreshment; my refuge and my help; my wisdom; my portion, my possession, and my treasure, in whom my mind and my heart may ever remain fixed and firm, and rooted inmmovably, henceforth and for evermore. Amen. (One year's Indulgence.)

Another Prayer of St. Thomas Aquinas

Almighty and Everlasting God, the Preserver of souls and the Redeemer of the world, look favorably upon me, Thy servant, prostrate before Thy Majesty, and most graciously accept this Sacrifice, which I have offered, in honor of Thy name, for the saving health of the faithful, living as well as departed, as also for all my sins and offences. Take away Thine anger from me: grant Thy grace and mercy unto me; open unto me the gates of Paradise; deliver me by Thy power from all evils; and whatever guilt I have incurred of my own sinfulness, do Thou graciously forgive; and make me so to persevere in Thy precepts in this world, that I may be rendered worthy to be joined to the company of Thy elect; of Thine only gift, O my God, whose blessed name, honor, and dominion endureth for ever and ever. Amen.

Aspirations of St. Ignatius

Soul of Christ sanctify me.
Body of Christ, save me.
Blood of Christ, inebriate me.
Water from the side of Christ, wash me,
Passion of Christ, strengthen me.
O good Jesus, hear me.
Within Thy wounds hide me.
Permit me not to be separated from Thee.
From the malignant enemy defend me.
In the hour of my death call me.
And bid me come to Thee,
That, with Thy saints, I may praise Thee.
For ever and ever. Amen.

(300 days' Indulgence.)

Oblation of St. Ignatius

Take, O Lord, and receive my entire liberty, my memory, my understanding, and all my will. All that I am, all that I have, Thou hast given me, and I give it back again to Thee, to be disposed of according to Thy good pleasure. Give me only Thy love and Thy grace; with these I am rich enough, nor do I ask for aught besides. (300 days' Indulgence.)

Prayer to Jesus Crucified

Look down upon me, good and gentle Jesus, while before Thy face I humbly kneel, and with burning soul pray and beseech Thee to fix deep in my heart lively sentiments of Faith, Hope, and Charity, true contrition for my sins, and a firm purpose of amendment; while I contemplate with great love and tender pity Thy five wounds, pondering over them within me, and calling to mind what the prophet David put in Thy mouth concerning Thee, O good Jesus: "They have pierced my hands and my feet; they have numbered all my bones."

(Plenary Indulgence when recited before an image of Christ Crucified after confession and Communion, when followed by the usual prayers for the intention of the Holy Father.)

Prayer to Our Lord Jesus Christ

I beseech Thee, O sweetest Lord Jesus Christ, that Thy Passion may be for me a power of strength, protection, and defence, that Thy Wounds may be for me food and drink by which I may be fed, inebriated, and delighted: the sprinkling of Thy Blood may impart to me the remission of all my sins: Thy death may be to me life eternal. May they be to me nourishment, courage, health and sweetness of heart: Who livest and reignest for ever and ever. Amen. (When recited after Mass, Indulgence of three years.)

Prayer to the Blessed Virgin

O Mary, most holy virgin and Mother, behold, I have received thy most beloved Son, who thou didst conceive in thy immaculate womb, bear, nourish, and caress with tenderest embraces. Behold, Him, in whose presence thou rejoicest, and art filled with all sweetness, I humbly and lovingly offer and present to thy embraces, to be loved by thy heart, and to be offered to the Most Adorable Trinity in profound adoration, for thy honor and glory, and for my necessities and those of the entire world. I therefore beseech thee, O most pious Mother, to obtain pardon for all my sins, abundance of grace to serve Him more faithfully in the future, and finally the grace of perseverance, so that, in union with thee, I may praise Him for ever and ever. Amen. (100 days' indulgence.)

Prayer of St. Augustine to the Blessed Virgin

O Most holy, O most fair and renowned, glorious Virgin Mary, who alone wert worthy to bear the Creator of all creatures in thy most holy womb, and to nourish Him at thy breasts: I, a miserable sinner, who have just presumed to receive His real and sacred Body and Blood, humbly implore thy mercy; deign to intercede for me a sinner with thy divine Son; so that whatever I have done unworthily in offering this ineffable and most sublime Sacrifice, whether by action or omission, through ignorance or neglect, through accident or irreverence, in receiving the same Lord Jesus Christ, thy Son, may deign to pardon through thy prayers: Who, with the Father and the Holy Spirit, liveth and reigneth for ever and ever. Amen.

Prayer to St. Joseph

O Guardian of Virgins, holy Father St. Joseph, to whose faithful protection Jesus (Innocence Itself), and Mary, the Virgin of virgins, were entrusted: I beseech and entreat thee by this double and most precious pledge of Jesus and Mary, that, preserved from all uncleanness, pure in heart, and chaste in body, thou wilt always make me serve Jesus and Mary most chastely. Amen. (100 days' indulgence.)

MANNER OF SERVING AT MASS

A. Special Notes

1. *The Latin.* Every server should know the prayers and responses by heart. However, until he does know them by heart, there is nothing shameful about reading them. In this case he should hold the card in his hand. He should not try to read it when it is resting on the floor or step. In any case the words should be carefully pronounced slowly.

2. *The Server's Appearance.* The server who is conscious of his high dignity at being allowed to approach so near to the Holy of Holies, will take proper care of his appearance.

(*a*) He should always wear *black* shoes, carefully cleaned and polished.

(*b*) His hair should be neatly combed.

(*c*) His cassock, besides being clean, should always be *long* enough to reach within four inches of the floor. A boy's stockings or trousers should never be visible beneath the cassock.

(*d*) The Surplice should be kept perfectly clean and neat. It must be washed and ironed frequently. Like the cassock it must never be too small. The proper length of a surplice is to the knees. If it does not reach the knees, at the very least it should come below the hips. It should be made entirely of linen, but if this is too expensive, lawn or broadcloth will satisfy, but never cotton. The sleeves of the surplice should be long and full, reaching to the *wrists*.

3. *The Server's Decorum.* The server's conduct can greatly add to or detract from the beauty and dignity of the Mass. Hence he should strive to move about with reverence and without haste. In spite of natural awkwardness he can do a great deal by avoid-

ing haste. If he realizes at all, and keeps before his mind the sanctity of the place, his decorum will befit the ceremony.

(a) *Hands.* Whether he be standing, kneeling, or walking,—when he is not carrying anything,—his hands should be joined palm to palm at the breast, fingers up, with the right thumb crossing the left. When he *is* carrying something, unless it requires two hands, he carries it with the right,—and his left hand lies flat on his breast.

(b) *Kneeling.* He kneels a good part of the time. In this posture he should normally be erect, with head up, hands joined at the breast, eyes and mind intent on the Mystery.

(c) *Standing.* In this position also he should be careful not to lean the weight on one foot more than another. His hands should be joined at the breast, head erect, eyes forward. He should be careful that he does not appear stiff or soldier-like.

(d) *Walking.* He should walk easily, neither too fast nor too slowly, hands joined, being careful to avoid any eccentricity of gait acquired elsewhere. About three paces should separate priest and server in going to and from the altar.

4. *The Server's Actions.* Each of the following ceremonial actions should be performed at the proper time with ease and assurance.

(a) *Bows. A. While standing.* There are only five bows that the Server is supposed to make while standing. In each of these cases the bow consists of a slight inclination of the *head*, done in a graceful manner, not jerkily. The shoulders do not move, nor do the hips. The five bows are:

1. When the server leaves the Missal after bringing it over for the Gospel.

2. At the Offertory when the Celebrant approaches to pour wine and water into the Chalice.

3. Immediately after this, before the server turns to bring the cruets back.

4 and 5. At the Lavabo the server makes the same two bows as at 2 and 3. *There are no others.*

B. *While kneeling.*

1. After the priest's Confiteor the server bows low towards the priest during the "Misereatur tui"; then he turns straight, but still bowing low until after his Confiteor and the priest's "Misereatur vestri." When the server says "Amen" he kneels erect again. Bowing "low" means to incline both head and shoulders.

2. During the versicles beginning "Deus tu conversus" etc., the server bows his head,—not the shoulders this time,—and raises it only at the word "Oremus," the last before the priest ascends the steps.

3. If the Credo is said, the server bows *low* at the words "Et incarnatus est," etc., during the priest's genuflection.

4. At the "Orate fratres"—*after* the priest has turned back to the altar again, the server bows *slightly*, just the head, and in that position says the prayer "Suscipiat." At its conclusion he kneels erect.

5. The server bows *low* four times during the Consecration, i.e., at the four genuflections of the priest. At each elevation he kneels erect and looks reverently upon the Blessed Sacrament.

6. He bows *slightly* when the priest consumes the Sacred Host.

7. He bows *low* when he says the Confiteor before Holy Communion.

8. The bows in the Sacristy to the Crucifix and to the priest, are *slight* bows.

(b) *Genuflections.* A genuflection is performed by allowing the right knee to touch the floor near the left foot. The body should always be directly pointed towards the object of reverence. A "sideways" genuflection indicates a careless person and the influence of thoughtless routine. The head and shoulders should always remain erect during a genuflection. It is affectatious to bend over abjectly. The descending and ascending movements should be evenly done, without haste or excessive slowness. The server never genuflects on the step.

(c) *Prostrations.* A prostration is made by going on both knees and making a *slight* bow. Only after raising the head should one stand.

(d) *Striking the Breast.* This is done with the ends of the fingers of the right hand while the left rests flat against the lower part of the breast; not affectedly as though waving, nor with a thump—but evenly and with a gentle stroke on the breast above the left hand. It is not done with the closed fist. The server should *not* strike his breast when the priest is saying "mea culpa," nor later during the "Domine non sum dignus" when he rings the bell; but he should do so at the repetition of these words before his own Communion. He should also strike his breast three times during the "Agnus Dei" at the words "miserere nobis" (twice) and "dona nobis pacem." He should not strike his breast at the words "O clement, O loving, O sweet Virgin Mary" during the "Salve Regina."

(e) *The Liturgical Kiss.* This is an act of reverence which illustrates the great respect which the Church has for even the inanimate objejcts which are used in the Great Sacrifice. The priest is directed to kiss the Altar frequently because the Holy Sacrifice is offered upon it. Thus also he kisses the Paten, the first words of the Gospel, and certain vestments which he wears,—all because they have reference to the Great Mystery. Hence the server is directed to kiss the cruet of wine, because some of the wine will become the Blood of Christ; and the cruet of water, because a few drops of it will be mingled with the wine in the Chalice. Again he kisses both of these after receiving them from the priest, because he who is to perform the rite of Sacrifice has touched these instruments. *Note*, however, that the liturgical kiss is a mere touching of the *closed lips* to the object. It is done simply and reverently without noise.

(*f*) *Pouring Wine or Water*. Some boys are much too slow in pouring wine and water. They let it fall drop by drop. Others much to careless and spill it over the fingers in and around the Chalice in great cataracts. Please remember that the priest does not wish to speak to anyone at these moments. He is engaged with the prayers of the "Lavabo" or those of the Ablutions, and therefore cannot readily direct. Judge the flow of wine or water so that it comes neither too slowly nor too quickly.

1. At the Lavabo the priest washes merely the thumb and forefinger of each hand, and only the tips of these. Therefore do not try to pour water over any other part of his hands.

2. At the Ablutions when the server steps to the side of the priest to pour wine into the Chalice he should pour rather freely, but should be careful to avoid splashing.

3. A moment later he pours but a very *small* quantity of wine, and *much* water over the priest's fingers into the Chalice. He should remember that both wine and water should be poured on the fingers to wash them, and should not seek an opening to pour between them. Likewise it is not necessary for the server to pour with a circling motion as if to include the whole finger. There is danger of spilling.

(g) *The Missal.* The server is never allowed at Low Mass to open or close the Missal, or to turn its pages.

B Serving on the Side Altars

Serving at the side altars is the same as serving at the main altar with these special things to be observed:

1. In going to and from a side altar a genuflection is made in the direction of the main altar when passing. In the event that priest and server pass the main altar while Mass is going on at that altar, the genuflection occurs as just mentioned. If the priest at the main altar is distributing Holy Communion a genuflection on both knees must be made before rising and passing on. But if the priest celebrating at the main altar is at the Consecration of the Mass, anyone passing to or fro must kneel on both knees for the end of the Consecration before rising and passing on.

2. When priest and server arrive at the designated side altar, the priest will *bow*, but the server *must genuflect*. This is true all during the Mass and at the end just before leaving. The server never bows at the center, but always genuflects toward the Crucifix when passing the middle of the altar.

3. Since the credence table is close to each one of the side altars, the movements of the server will be more simple during the Offertory and Ablutions, but they are essentially the same as at the main altar.

4. The bell is never rung at the side altars.

5. Since there is no bench at the side altars, the priest's biretta should be put on the lower shelf of the credence table.

6. Holy Communion is not regularly given out at the side altars. The server will receive during the general administration of Holy Communion from the main altar.

7. The server must always be on the priest's right when receiving or giving the biretta. In this position he will be nearer the Sacristy at the end of Mass at both the altars in Our Lady's Chapel, but not at the farther altar in St Joseph's Chapel. Here after the last genuflection he must quickly step around the priest to precede him to the Sacristy.

C. At the Main Altar

1. *Preparation.* The Server must remember always that he should not keep the priest waiting. He should come to the Sacristy, therefore, with the priest, put on his cassock and surplice quickly, see that the candles are lighted and the cruets filled. He should then stand near the priest, while he is vesting, to be of service if necessary.

2. *Procession.* When the priest puts on his biretta and takes the Chalice in his hand, the server bows with him to the Crucifix, and precedes him to the altar, walking erect and reverently, neither too fast nor too slowly, with hands joined at the breast. The entrance to the Sanctuary on the Gospel side is used. The server goes immediately, without genuflecting, to the Epistle side of the altar, so as to be on the priest's right when he arrives. The server genuflects with him, and receives his biretta. He rises immediately and assists the priest to ascend the steps by raising the front of his alb a trifle. Then he brings the priest's biretta to the bench and returns, genuflects at the middle, and goes to the Gospel side, where he *kneels* on the floor about a foot to the left of where the priest will stand. Kneeling, he waits for the priest to descend.

3 *At the Foot of the Altar.* During tne prayers at the foot of the altar the server must be careful to bless himself whenever the priest does. He should

bow his head slightly at the "Gloria Patri," but should not bow his head or strike his breast during the priest's Confiteor. During the priest's Confiteor the server kneels erect, but at its conclusion he bows low and turning slightly toward the priest, says the "Misereatur tui." When the priest replies "Amen," the server turns to the altar again, still bowing low, and says the Confiteor, turning toward the priest again at the words "et tibi, pater" and "et te, pater," The server does not kneel erect again until he says "Amen" to the "Misereatur vestri," etc., of the priest. He bows his head slightly, and remains in that position during the Versicles "Deus tu conversus," etc., until the priest says "Oremus" and begins to ascend the steps.

4. *Up to the Gospel.* The Server rises at the word "Oremus" and assists the priest to ascend the steps by raising the front of his alb a trifle. (He does not go up the steps with the priest.) Then, without genuflecting, he kneels on the first step, on the Gospel side. As Mass continues the Server always blesses himself when the priest does. He makes all the necessary responses as usual, and at the priest's signal, says "Deo gratias" at the end of the Epistle. He rises, genuflects at the center, walks around on the floor of the Sanctuary to the right of the priest, and waits at the top step for the priest to finish. When the priest leaves the book and walks to the center, the server takes it, without bowing, goes down the steps diagonally to the middle, genuflects on the floor, ascends the steps and deposits the book at the Gospel corner of the altar, slantwise. He steps down from the footpace, and stands by the book, facing it. He makes the necessary responses when the priest begins, makes the sign of the cross on the forehead, lips and breast as the priest does, and bows *slightly* at the name of Our Lord which usually occurs in the first sentence of the Gospel.

Only then does he leave, turning to his left to descend to the floor, then turning to his right to walk to the middle. There he genuflects, goes to the Epistle side, and turns to face *toward the priest* while he reads the Gospel. When the priest finishes the Gospel, the server says "Laus tibi, Christe" immediately, and *kneels*. He remains *kneeling* through the Credo if this follows, bowing low when the priest genuflects at the words "Et incarnatus est," etc. He answers the "Dominus vobiscum" still kneeling.

5. *The Offertory*. When the priest finishes the Offertory verse and removes the Chalice' veil, the the Server rises and turning to his right, goes *without genuflecting*, to the credence table. Taking the wine cruet in his right hand and the water cruet in his left, and holding them by the *bottom* so that the priest may grasp each by the handle, he goes to the top step of the altar at the Epistle side, and stands there *facing* the priest. As the priest comes toward him, the Server bows slightly and presents the wine cruet after having *kissed* it. Then he transfers the water cruet to the right hand and kisses it. This he presents to the priest after having received the wine cruet. He kisses the wine cruet, and also the water cruet when the priest returns them. (NOTE: these four kisses are omitted at a Reqium Mass.) The server stands there *facing* the priest, until he turns with the Chalice and bows towards the Crucifix. The server bows with him slightly—*towards the Crucifix*, then turning to his right goes back to the credence table, where he deposits the cruets, and covers the wine cruet. He puts the towel on his left forearm, takes the bowl in his left hand and the water cruet in his right hand, and goes to the altar again. He stands at the top step *facing* the priest, and when he approaches, the Server bows slightly and pours—not too slowly—a sufficient

amount of water over the priest's thumb and forefinger of each hand. Then he turns to his right so that the priest can take the towel more easily from his forearm, and in that position he waits until the priest gives back the towel. With him he bows slightly to the *Crucifix* and turning to the right goes to the credence table, where he deposits bowl, cruet and towel. After covering the cruet and folding the towel neatly, he turns to the left, and retraces his steps to his place on the *Epistle* side, *without genuflecting*. When the priest says "Orate fratres" the server waits until the priest *faces the altar* before beginning the prayer "Suscipiat," etc. Then bowing slightly he says this prayer distinctly at his place on the Epistle side, and kneels erect again at its conclusion.

6. *The Preface.* He makes the necessary responses to the Preface and at its conclusion rings the bell three times during the words "Sanctus, Sanctus, Sanctus." He rings it once only when the priest spreads his hands over the Chalice. Then rising, he mounts the steps and kneels on the footpace a little to the right of the priest but near enough to raise the end of his chasuble during the elevation. When the priest genuflects, the server bows low, then kneels erect and raises *slightly* the end of the priest's chasuble as he elevates the Host. The server then releases the Chasuble, and bows as the priest repeats his genuflection. These actions are repeated at the Elevation of the Chalice. Meanwhile he rings the bell at each action—six times in all. (NOTE 1:—when the bell is so large that it cannot be carried, the server will remain near it, not assisting with the Chasuble, NOTE 2:—the Chasuble is not to be lifted during the priest's genuflections, but only at the actual elevation, to give him more freedom in raising his arms.) After the Elevation of the Chalice and the priest's last genu-

flection, the Server rises, turns to the left, and descends to the floor. He genuflects at the middle and returns to his place at the Epistle side. Here he remains, making the necessary responses. He strikes his breast with the priest at the "Agnus Dei." He does not do so at the "Domine, non sum dignus" before the *priest's* Communion, but rings the bell three times. While the priest consumes the Sacred Host, the server bows reverently.

7. *The Communion.* A. *When the Server and Others Will Receive.* At the priest's genuflection a moment later, the server, at his own place, must be ready to genuflect with him. Then he goes to the Epistle corner of the altar with the Communion plate. He kneels on the footpace, and when the priest makes the sign of the Cross with the Chalice. the server, bowing low, says the Confiteor. He answers the two versicles which follow, and strikes his breast three times at the "Domine, non sum dignus" which follows. The priest then comes to him with the Blessed Sacrament, and after the server has received, he must rise immediately and, without genuflecting, go by the shortest way to the first person who is to receive, and present him with the plate. Here the server returns to his place at the Epistle side where he kneels facing the altar. No genuflection is necessary as he approaches his place. Kneeling here he makes his thanksgiving until the priest returns. Only after the Tabernacle door is closed does he rise, and *without genuflecting,* go to the credence table for the cruets.

B. *When the Server Alone Receives.*

Everything as given above. When he has received, he gives the plate to the priest, and pausing long enough to swallow the Sacred Host, he rises, (after the Tabernacle door has been closed) turns to his right and goes to the credence table for the cruets.

C. *When No One is to Receive.*

While the priest consumes the Sacred Host, the server bows reverently. At the priests's genuflection a moment later, the server must be ready *at his own place* to genuflect with him. Then he goes to the credence table for the cruets.

8. *The Ablutions.* He returns with the cruets to the Epistle corner of the altar. If no one has received, the priest will *not* have consumed the Precious Blood. In this case the server genuflects toward the center of the altar before ascending the steps. But if even one person has received, the priest will have already consumed the Precious Blood, and there is no need for the server to genuflect. He waits on the top step facing the priest, until he holds the Chalice towards him. Immediately the server steps up on the footpace, walks near enough to avoid awkward stretching, and pours into the Chalice a certain amount of wine. In pouring the wine he must carefully avoid touching the Chalice either with the cruet or with his fingers. To avoid awkwardness he should hold the cruet by the base and side when pouring, *not by the handle.* When the priest has signified by a slight movement of the Chalice that he has poured enough, the server stops deftly, in such a way as to prevent the wine from spilling. This is *not* done by scraping the cruet on the edge of the Chalice! Turning to his right he steps down from the footpace to the top step where he turns back again to face the priest. When the priest presents the Chalice this time, it is to purify his fingers. The Server therefore, pours a small quantity of wine and a larger quantity of water in turn over the fingers of the priest into the Chalice. This pouring is done in both cases by the right hand. *The Server never pours with the left.* After pouring the small quantity of wine he slips the looped handle on the

little finger of his left hand. Then taking the water cruet with his right, he pours almost all of it over the priest's fingers, as was said above. He must take care *never* to let the cruets *touch the priest's fingers*. Then, *without bowing*, he turns to the right and goes to the credence table, where he deposits and covers the cruets.

9. *Changing the Book.* Turning by his left at the credence table, the server comes to the middle, genuflects, goes up the steps to the Gospel side, takes the book, goes down to the middle again, genuflects, and brings it up to the Epistle side. He deposits the Book, *not slantwise*, but straight, parallel to the edge of the altar. Then he takes the Chalice Veil from the altar near the Book, unfolds it, and standing where he is on the priest's *right*, waits there until he is ready for it. Then after handing it to him by the upper corners, he turns to his left, *without bowing*, and descends to the middle, genuflects and goes to his place on the Gospel side, where he kneels erect. Here he answers the prayers, and *here* he receives the blessing. He answers "Amen" to the blessing, and rises. Standing there he answers the versicles to the Last Gospel. Only after saying "Gloria tibi, Domine," does he move to the right. He genuflects at the middle, goes to the bench for the biretta, takes it in both hands, resting it on his breast, and comes to place on the Epistle side where he awaits the genuflection occurring in the Last Gospel. He genuflects with the priest, answers "Deo gratias" at the end, and waits for the priest to descend. He kneels with him on the first step, *not on the floor*.

10. *Special Last Gospel.* If the Book remains open on the Epistle side after the "Ite, missa est," the server rises after answering this versicle, genuflects in the middle, ascends the steps, takes the Book, descends the steps, and kneels on the first step at the

middle until the priest gives the blessing. Replying "Amen" he rises, and brings the Book to the Gospel side, where, on the top step, he answers the versicles, and bows toward the Book if the Name of Our Lord occurs in the first sentence. Turning to his left, he descends to the floor, then turning to his right he walks to the center, genuflects, goes for the biretta and returns without genuflecting to his place on the Epistle side. He says "Deo gratias" at the end, waits for the priest to descend, and kneels with him on the first step.

11. *Recession.* After the prayers at the end of Mass, the server rises with the priest; waits till he descends again with the Chalice, (or if he has it with him already), genuflects, hands him the biretta *by the front peak,* so that the priest can grasp the *middle one,* turns and leads him slowly to the Sacristy by the door on the Epistle side, precedes him to the Vestment Case, bows with him toward the Crucifix, then bows towards the priest. He then sees to it that the cruets are changed and the candles extinguished if no other Mass is to follow. If another Mass is to follow, he merely changes the cruets.

[*Contributed by T. F. D.*]

SERVING AT MASS

Priest. † In nomine Patris, et Filii, et Spiritus Sancti.
Server. Amen.

P. Introibo ad altare Dei.

S. Ad Deum, qui laetificat juventutem meam.

P. Judica me, Deus, et discerne causam meam de gente, non sancta, ab homine iniquo et doloso erue me.

S. Quia tu es, Deus, fortitudo mea, quare me repulisti, et quare tristis incedo, dum affligit me inimicus?

P. Emitte lucem tuam et veritatem tuam; inpsa me deduxerunt et adduxerunt in montem sanctum tuum, et in tabernacula tua.

S. Et introibo ad altare Dei, ad Deum, qui laetificat juventutem meam.

P. Confitebor tibi in cithara, Deus, Deus meus; quare tristis es anima mea, et quare conturbas me?

S. Spera in Deo, quoniam adhuc confitebor illi: salutare vultus mei, et Deus meus.

P. Gloria Patri, et Filio, et Spiritu Sancto.

S. Sicut erat in principio, et nunc, et semper, et in saecula saeculorum. Amen.

P. Introibo ad altare Dei.

S. Ad Deum, qui laetificat juventutem meam.

P. Adjutorium nostrum in nomine Domini.

S. Qui fecit coelum et terram.

P. Confiteor Deo, etc.

Bow the head when the Priest begins this, and continue bent until you have finished the Confiteor.

S. Misereatur tui omnipotens Deus, et dimissis peccatis tuis, perducat te ad vitam aeternam.

P. Amen.

S. Confiteor Deo omnipotenti, beatae Mariae semper Virgini, beato Michaeli Archangelo, beato Joanni Baptistae, Sanctis Apostolis Petro et Paulo, omnibus Sanctis, et tibi, Pater, (*here turn your head toward the Priest and then go on*), quia peccavi nimis cogitatione, verbo et opere, (*striking your breast thrice*), mea culpa, mea culpa, mea maxima culpa. Ideo precor beatam Mariam semper Virginem, beatum Michaelem Archangelum, beatum Joannem Baptistam, Sanctos Apostolos Petrum et Paulum, omnes Sanctos,

et te, Pater, (*here turn again toward the Priest*), orare pro me ad Dominum Deum nostrum.
- P. Misereatur vestri, etc.
- S. Amen.
- P. Indulgentiam, absolutionem, etc.
- S. Amen.
- P. Deus tu conversus, vivificabis nos.
- S. Et plebs tua laetabitur in te.
- P. Ostende nobis, Domine, misericordiam tuam.
- S. Et salutare tuum da nobis.
- P. Domine, exaudi orationem meam.
- S. Et clamor meus ad te veniat.
- P. Dominus vobiscum.
- S. Et cum spiritu tuo.
- P. Kyrie eleison.
- S. Kyrie eleison.
- P. Kyrie eleison.
- S. Christe eleison.
- P. Chiste eleison.
- S. Christe eleison.
- P. Kyrie eleison.
- S. Kyrie eleison.
- P. Kyrie eleison.

After the Gloria, or when it is omitted, after the Kyrie:
- P. Dominus vobiscum.
- S. Et cum spiritu tuo.

At the end of the prayer Oremus:
- P. Per omnia saecula saeculorum.
- S. Amen.

At the end of Epistle say: Deo gratias.
- P. Dominus vobiscum.
- S. Et cum spiritu tuo.
- P. Sequentia sancti, etc.

Here make the sign of the Cross: 1. *Upon your forehead*. 2. *Upon your mouth*. 3. *Upon your breast, and say*: Gloria tibi, Domine.

At the end of the Gospel, say:

S. Laus tibi, Christe.

At the words in the Creed, et incarnatus, *etc., kneel.*

P. Dominus vobiscum.

S. Et cum spiritu tuo.

P. Orate fratres, etc.

S. Suscipiat Dominus sacrificium de manibus tuis, ad laudem et gloriam nominis sui, ad utilitatem quoque nostram, totiusque Ecclesiae suae sanctae.

P. Per omnia saecula saeculorum.

S. Amen.

P. Dominus vobiscum.

S. Et cum spiritu tuo.

P. Sursum corda.

S. Habemus ad Dominum.

P. Gratias agamus Domino Deo nostro.

S. Dignum et justum est.

P. Per omnia saecula saeculorum.

S. Amen.

P. Et ne nos inducas in tentationem.

S. Sed libera nos a malo.

P. Per omnia saecula saeculorum.

S. Amen.

P. Pax Domini sit semper vobiscum.

S. Et cum spiritu tuo.

P. Dominus vobiscum.

S. Et cum spiritu tuo.

P. Per omnia saecula saeculorum.

S. Amen.

P. Dominus vobiscum.

S. Et cum spiritu tuo.

P. Ite missa est; *or* Benedicamus Domino.

S. Deo gratias.

Note.—In Masses for the dead the Priest says:

P. Requiescant in pace.
S. Amen.

If the book be left open, remove it to the Gospel side. Kneel in the middle of the altar to receive the Priest's blessing.

Note.—In Masses for the dead the blessing is not given.

P. Pater, et Filius, et Spiritus Sanctus.
S. Amen.

Then rise.

P. Dominus vobiscum.
S. Et cum spiritu tuo.
P. Initium; *or* Sequentia sancti Evangelii secundum etc.
S. Gloria tibi Domine.

At the end of the Gospel, say:

Deo gratias.

The Society for the Propagation of the Faith

In the year 1822 a woman in France conceived the idea of enlisting memberships in a Society which would have as its purpose the spreading of the Faith throughout the world. It crystalized in a movement which was endorsed by Rome, and it was formally approved by Rome as "The Society for the Propagation of the Faith." The new American Republic became one of the first beneficiaries of the funds collected by it.

Today this Society is established in every Christian country, and offers the principal support to Missionary Priests, Sisters and Brothers at work in all pagan lands.

In the United States memberships were solicited on the basis of 5c the month, and since the close of the World War catholics of this country have contributed as much as all the rest of the world combined. The National Director of the Society in the United States is a member of the Council which meets in Rome at regular intervals for the distribution of the funds. Perpetual memberships for the benefit of foreign missions are $40.00.

In the year 1924 the American Episcopate received the approval of the Holy See to raise the membership fee in the United States to $1.00 the year, in order that 40c from each member might be devoted to the Missions under the American Flag.

At present the Society is known here as the "Society for the Propagation of the Faith for Home and Foreign Missions," and has been introduced into most dioceses. Of the funds collected 60% are sent to the New York Office of the Propagation of the Faith for Foreign Missions, and 40% are sent to the Treasurer of the American Board of Catholic Missions for use in our own country.

The Holy Father has granted rich indulgences to all people who affiliate with this joint Society, and grants rare faculties to priests who introduce it and encourage it. Parish promoters write out memberships to every annual contributor of $1.00.

Members are asked to say daily the Our Father and Hail Mary, together with the invocation "St. Francis Xavier, pray for us."

The Catholic Church Extension Society

Organized in 1905 to assist the Home Missions of the United States, the Philippine Islands, Alaska and Porto Rico. Endorsed by the Holy Father and the American Hierarchy. Assists in building mission churches with donations of $1,000 or more, supplies mission churches with altars, stations of the cross, vestments, chalices, etc. Helps support missionary bishops and priests with subsidies and Mass Intentions. Educates poor students for the missionary priesthood. Supports two Chapel Cars in the mission field. Extension depends entirely upon the voluntary offerings of the faithful for its mission work. Publishes Extension Magazine, the official organ of the Home Missions. Archbishop of Chicago, by his office, presiding officer. Located at 180 North Wabash Avenue, Chicago, Illinois.

The Holy Childhood

The Association of the Holy Childhood is an auxiliary of the Society for the Propagation of the Faith. It is intended for children, from whom, after enrollment, it expects at least one cent the month, and on whom it imposes the easy spiritual burden of reciting once each day one "Hail Mary" and the invocation "Holy Virgin Mary, pray for us and poor pagan children." Perpetual memberships are $25.00.

This Society, started in 1830 by a few students in Paris, has grown to great proportions. Its members are usually united in Parish Conferences, and assist the needy both by money and service, visit the sick, distribute good literature, etc.

The Missionary Union of the Clergy increases the interest of clerics in major orders in the missions. Interest in the establishment of a native clergy in mission lands is of utmost importance also.

AMERICAN MARTYRS

Isaac Jogues, born Orleans, France, Jan. 10, 1607; Jesuit, 1626; priest, 1636; missionary among Hurons, Canada, 1636-42; prisoner tortured and enslaved by Iroquois, Auriesville, N. Y., 1642-43; peacemaker with Iroquois, May, 1646; missionary to Iroquois, Oct. 1646; martyred by them, Oct. 18, 1646.

Rene Goupil, born Angers, France, about 1612; forced by illness to leave Jesuit novitiate; studied surgery; devoted life to Huron missionaries; taken prisoner by Iroquois with Jogues; tomahawked by them for teaching child Sign of Cross, Sept. 29, 1642. North America's first canonized martyr.

John Lalande, born Dieppe, France; devoted life to missionaries when very young; companion to Jogues on mission to Iroquois; put to death for loyalty to the missionary, Oct. 19, 1646.

John de Brebeuf, born Conde-sur-vire, France, March 25, 1593; Jesuit, 1616; priest, 1622; missionary among Montaignais and Hurons, 1625-29; forced by English to return to France, 1629-33; back to Hurons, 1633-49; tortured frightfully and put to death by Iroquois, March 16. 1649.

Gabriel Lalemant, born Paris, Oct. 10, 1610; Jesuit, 1630; priest, 1638; missionary to Hurons, 1646; tortured with and like Brebeuf, died March 17, 1649.

Anthony Daniel, born Dieppe, France, May 27, 1601; Jesuit, 1621; missonary, Cape Breton, 1632; Hurons, 1634; put to death by Iroquois, July 4, 1648.

Charles Garnier, born Paris, May 25, 1606; Jesuit, 1624; priest, 1635; missionary, 1636; put to death by Iroquois, Dec. 7 1649

Noel Chabanel, born Mende, France, Feb. 12, 1613; Jesuit, 1630; priest, 1641; missionary, 1643; put to death by apostate Huron, Dec. 8, 1649.

PRAYER

O God, who by the preaching and blood of Thy Blessed Martyrs, John and Isaac and their companions, didst consecrate the first fruits of the faith in the vast regions of North America, graciously grant that by their intercession the flourishing harvest of Christians may everywhere and always be increased. Through Our Lord Jesus Christ Thy Son who liveth and reigneth with Thee in union with the Holy Spirit, one God world without end. Amen

Imprimatur P. Cardinal Hayes

AN ACT OF CONSECRATION

[*The members of the Catholic Students Mission Crusade promise to aid the Missions by prayer, study of the Missions, or alms*]

I a knight of the Crusade, consecrate myself today to Jesus Christ, my King and Sovereign. I offer myself as a servant in this Holy War, the conquest of the world for the Sacred Heart. I will pray; I will sacrifice; I will serve that the Kingdom of Christ may be spread on earth. Christ Jesus, King of this new Crusade, accept my pledge of loyal service. Consecrate my heart by unselfishness, loyalty to Your cause, zeal for the conquest of the world. My motto: The Sacred Heart for the World! The World for the Sacred Heart!

www.ingramcontent.com/pod-product-compliance
Lightning Source LLC
Chambersburg PA
CBHW051714040426
42446CB00008B/880